LOYISOMKIZE**ART**

KWEZI™

COLLECTOR'S EDITION

© LOYISOMKIZEART (PTY)LTD (2014/15)

BIND-UP EDITION 2016
SEVENTH IMPRESSION 2023

PUBLISHED BY DAVID PHILIP PUBLISHERS (PTY) LTD
UNIT 13A, ATHLONE INDUSTRIAL PARK
10 MYMOENA CRESCENT, INDUSTRIA 2, NEWFIELDS
CAPE TOWN 7764
SOUTH AFRICA

ISBN: 978-1-4856-2272-7
E PUB ISBN: 978-1-4856-2273-4

COVER ART BY: LOYISO MKIZE
CREATOR/ILLUSTRATOR: LOYISO MKIZE
COLOURIST/CREATIVE CONSULTANT: CLYDE BEECH
KWEZI MARKETING: ROLIHLAHLA MHLANGA
KWEZI WEBSITE: PETER PHILLIP
KWEZI DESIGN: VIWE MFAKU

PRINTED BY: BIDVEST DATA

DAVID PHILIP IS COMMITTED TO A SUSTAINABLE FUTURE
FOR OUR BUSINESS, OUR READERS AND OUR COUNTRY.

KWEZI™ IS A PRODUCT OF LOYISOMKIZEART (PTY) LTD. ALL RIGHTS RESERVED. THE STORIES, CHARACTERS AND INCIDENTS MENTIONED IN THIS BOOK ARE ENTIRELY FICTIONAL. ALL CHARACTERS FEATURED IN THIS BOOK AND DISTINCTIVE LIKENESSES THEREOF ARE TRADEMARKS OF LOYISOMKIZEART (PTY). NO PART OF THIS PUBLICATION MAY BE REPRODUCED, STORED IN ANY RETRIEVAL SYSTEM OR BE TRANSMITTED IN ANY FORM OR BY ANY MEANS, ELECTRONIC OR MECHANICAL, WITHOUT PRIOR PERMISSION OF THE PUBLISHER. ANY PERSON WHO DOES ANY UNAUTHORISED ACT IN RELATION TO THIS PUBLICATION MAY BE LIABLE TO CRIMINAL PROSECUTUION AND CIVIL CLAIMS FOR DAMAGES.

MILLIONS OF YEARS AGO, THIS WORLD WAS AT ITS MOST HOSTILE. MEN WHO WALKED THE EARTH HAD REJECTED THEIR POTENTIAL TO CREATE, DEVELOP AND CO-EXIST BUT RATHER EMBRACED THE URGE TO DOMINATE AND DESTROY. WARS WERE MANY. DEATH WAS THE PRODUCT OF GREED AND POWER. MAN HAD BROUGHT HIMSELF TO THE EDGE OF EXTINCTION.

ON THE EVE OF MAN'S LAST MOMENTS ON THE EARTH, THE SKY LIT UP WITH A BRILLIANT LIGHT. A STAR UNLIKE ANY THEY HAD SEEN BEFORE. AND FOR ONCE THERE WAS A GREAT PAUSE AMONGST ALL MEN. A GREAT UNCERTAINTY FELL UPON ALL WHO SAW IT.

LATER THAT UNCERTAINTY WAS REPLACED WITH FEAR AS STRANGE THINGS BEGAN TO OCCUR. PEOPLE EVERYWHERE CLAIMED TO HAVE SEEN STRANGE BEINGS WHO LOOKED HUMAN BUT APPEARED TO HAVE BEEN LIT FROM INSIDE. THEY DISPLAYED INCREDIBLE **ABILITIES**.

THE WISE ONES ATTRIBUTED THIS TO THE EMERGENCE OF THE STAR, REPORTING THAT THESE SPECIAL PEOPLE WERE SOMEHOW CHOSEN BY THE STAR ITSELF. IT WAS BECAUSE OF THIS THAT THEY WERE THEN CALLED, **STAR PEOPLE**.

SOON THEY REALISED THAT THESE CHILDREN OF THE STAR WERE HERE TO HELP. THAT THEY WERE HERE TO HEAL THE WORLD.

AND THEY DID. YEARS PASSED AND THE STAR PEOPLE HAD NOT ONLY ADVANCED THE HUMANS, THEY HAD ALSO INSPIRED THEM.

WHEN THEIR WORK WAS DONE, THE STAR AND ITS CHOSEN DISAPPEARED. WHAT REMAINED WAS THE WORK THEY HAD DONE AND A GREAT MEMORY.

Panel 1:
"PUBLIC PERCEPTION SHOULD NOT BE HOW YOU MEASURE YOURSELF KWEZI. YOU HAVE ALWAYS DESPERATELY WANTED TO BE SEEN AND HEARD. IT IS WHY YOU RAN AWAY FROM HOME TO THE BIG CITY THOSE YEARS AGO.

AND NOW WITH THESE POWERS YOU FEEL THAT NAIVE AMBITION BECOMING A REALITY? THAT IS NOT WHY YOU YOU HAVE THESE POWERS MY BOY. THAT IS NOT YOUR PURPOSE."

Panel 2:
"NOT SO LONG AGO I WAS A NOBODY. AND NOW I'M DOING THINGS I NEVER EVEN DREAMT OF. YOU THINK BECAUSE YOU KNOW STUFF ABOUT ME, YOU CAN TELL ME WHAT TO DO NOW? YOU THINK I CAN'T HANDLE MYSELF?

I DONT NEED YOU! THIS IS MY LIFE, MY POWERS! NOT YOURS!"

Panel 3:
"KWEZI, PLEASE STOP!!"

"COMPANY. I HAVE LOST KWEZI. PROCEED WITH PURSUIT. BUT DO NOT HURT HIM, I REPEAT DON'T HURT HIM!!"

LOYISOMKIZEART
PRESENTS

KWEZI™

ISSUE #3

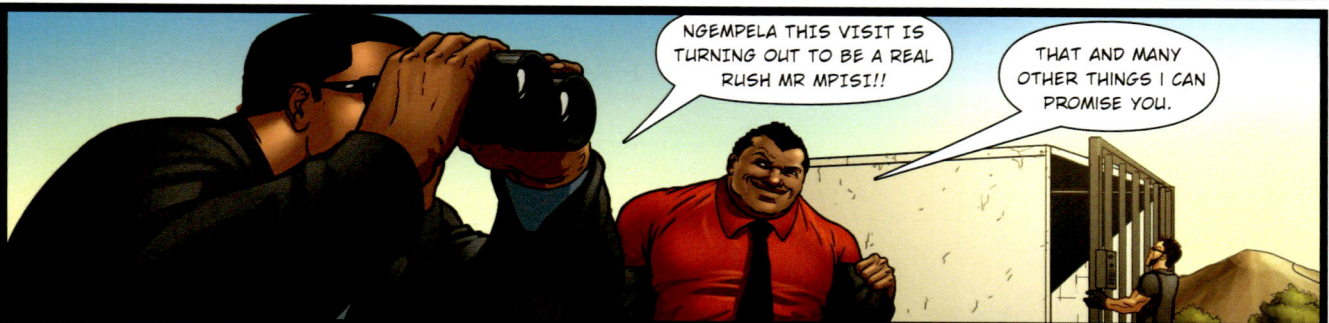

NGEMPELA THIS VISIT IS TURNING OUT TO BE A REAL RUSH MR MPISI!!

THAT AND MANY OTHER THINGS I CAN PROMISE YOU.

AMAZING. I NEVER KNEW UKUTHI INGONYAMA COULD PULL OFF A SOLO HUNT ON A ZEBRA LIKE THAT. **KING** OF THE JUNGLE!

KING?... I ALWAYS HAD A PROBLEM WITH THAT THEORY. IT ALWAYS SEEMED...

UNDISPUTED!

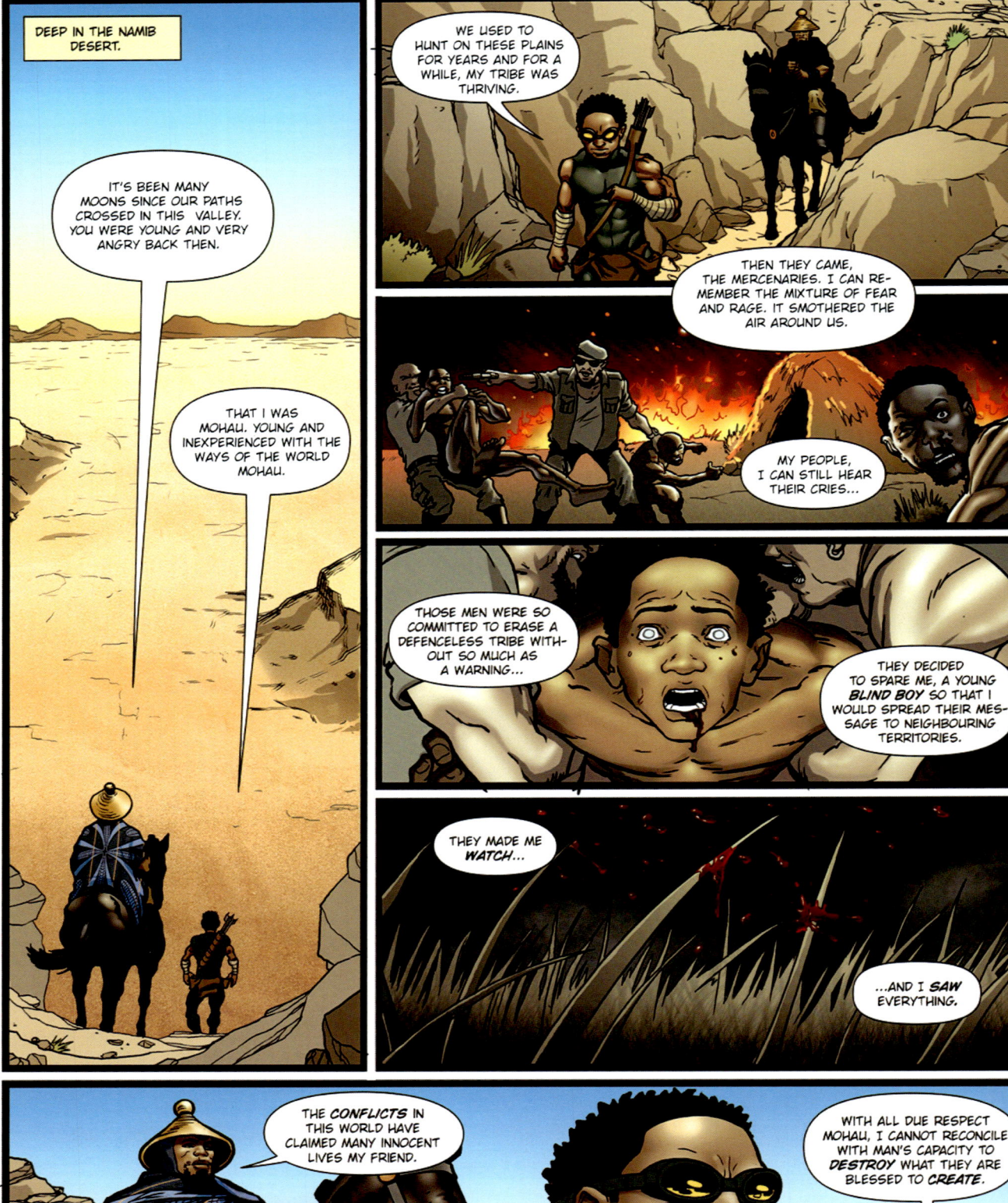

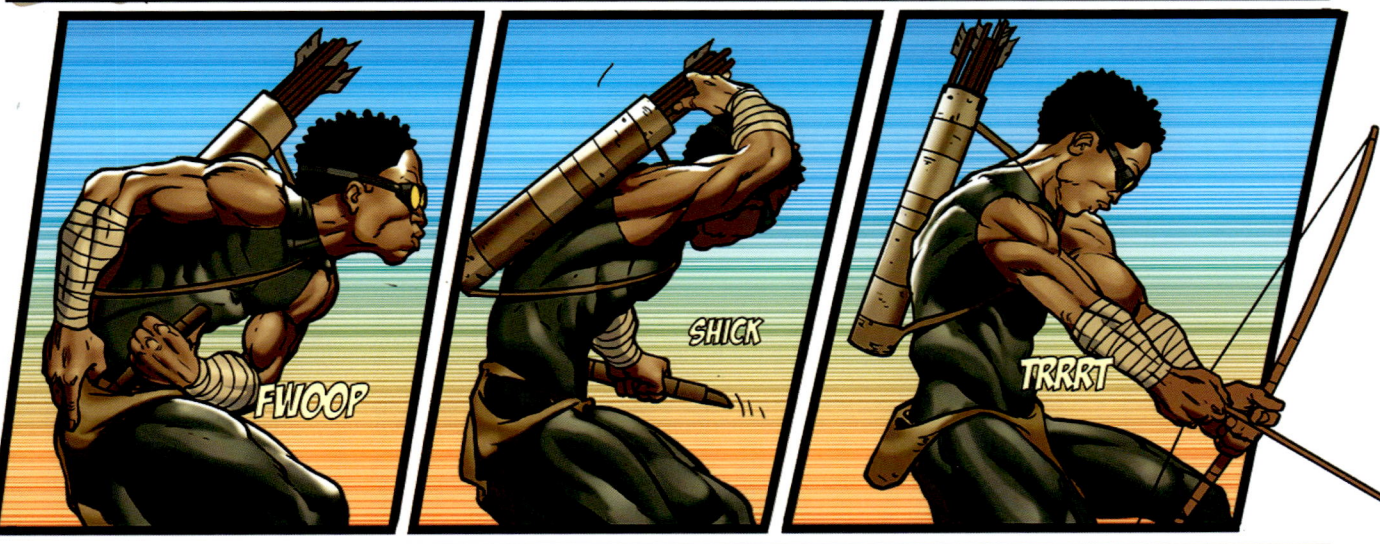

TEAM KWEZI

Loyiso Mkize was born in Butterworth and is now based in Cape Town. He is the founder of Loyiso Mkize Art and creator of Kwezi comics. As a visual artist, he has specialised both in Illustration and the fine arts. He has been in the comic book scene for nearly ten years and has been involved in numerous South African comic books. His fine arts career spans seven years with four solo exhibitions and six group exhibitions with a keen following both locally and internationally. He enjoys painting, reading comics and other books as well as engaging talks. He hopes his work will leave a lasting contribution to his industry, internationally.

Clyde Beech was born and bred in Cape Town. Even though things didn't quite work out for him in the beginning, once he got his foot in the door as a professional artist he managed to turn it into a career. At present he specialises as a comic book colorist, digital painter and art director. He has also had a stint in 2D animation as a background and texture artist. Being a geek, he loves comics, gaming and pop culture but that comes with a twist, he's also an avid martial artist. As a professional, his goal is to build a viable comic book industry for future artist in this country.